Let's Count Thanksgiving Things!

Are you ready? Let's Go!

HOW MANY SHIPS CAN YOU SEE?

1

11)

one

HOW MANY PINECONES CAN YOU SEE?

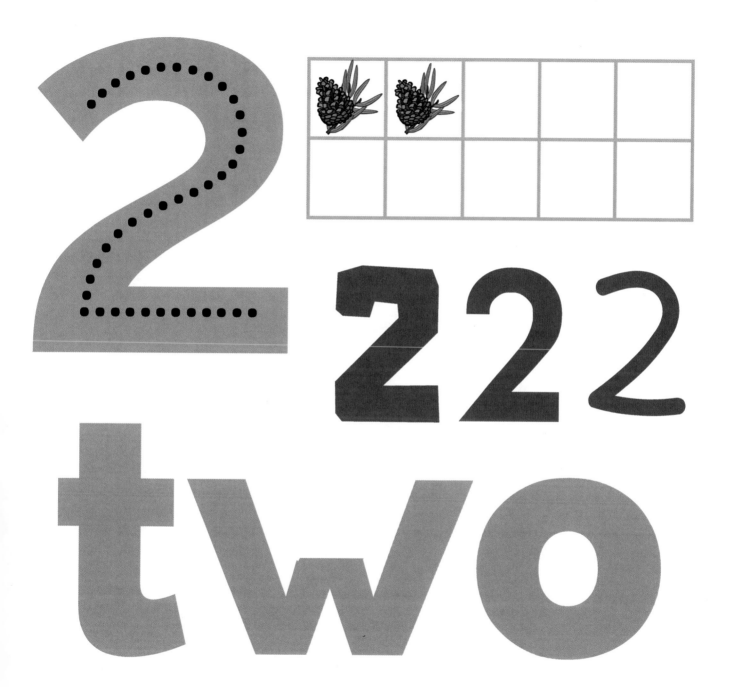

2

222

two

HOW MANY SCARECROWS CAN YOU SEE?

3

333

three

HOW MANY WAGONS CAN YOU SEE?

4

4 4 4 4

four

HOW MANY ACORNS CAN YOU SEE?

5

5 5 5 5

five

HOW MANY NATIVE AMERICANS CAN YOU SEE?

6 6 6 6

six

HOW MANY PIES CAN YOU SEE?

7

7 7 7 7

seven

HOW MANY FOXES CAN YOU SEE?

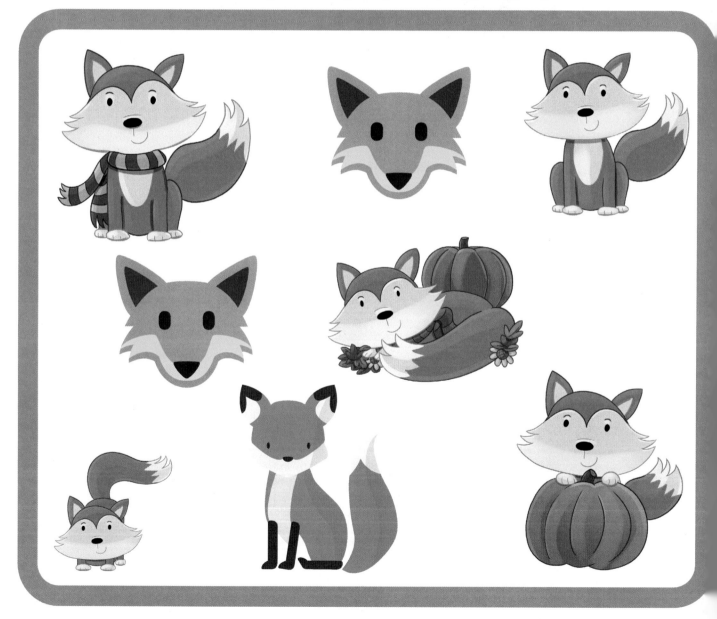

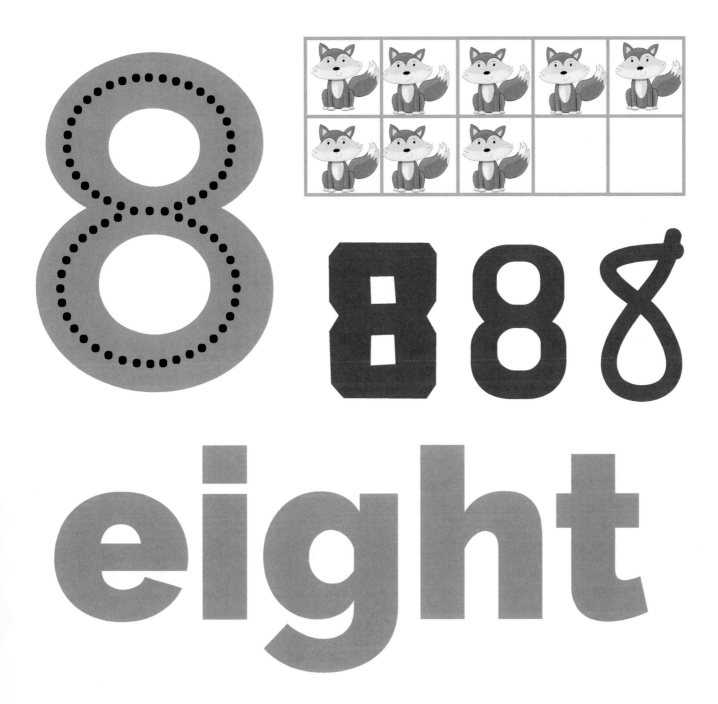

8

eight

HOW MANY FALL TREES CAN YOU SEE?

9

9 9 9 9

nine

HOW MANY OWLS CAN YOU SEE?

10

10 10 10

ten

HOW MANY COOKED TURKEYS CAN YOU SEE?

11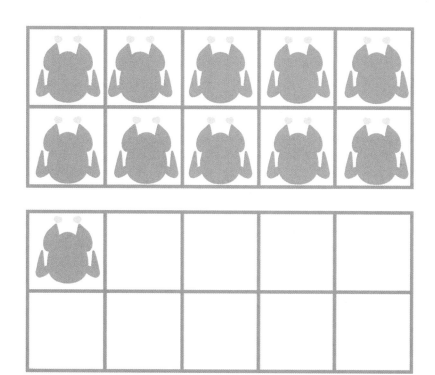

11 11 ||

eleven

HOW MANY PILGRIM HATS CAN YOU SEE?

12

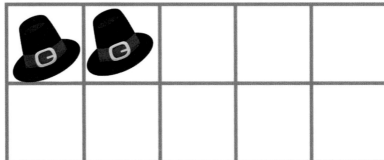

12 12 12

twelve

HOW MANY APPLE TREES CAN YOU SEE?

13

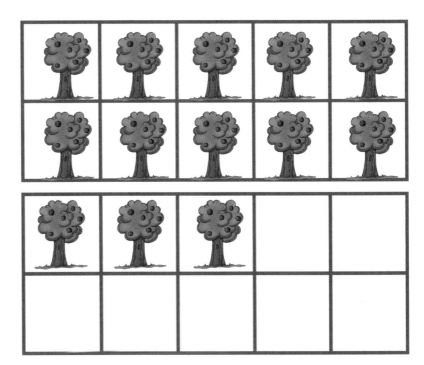

13 13 13

thirteen

HOW MANY TURKEYS CAN YOU SEE?

14

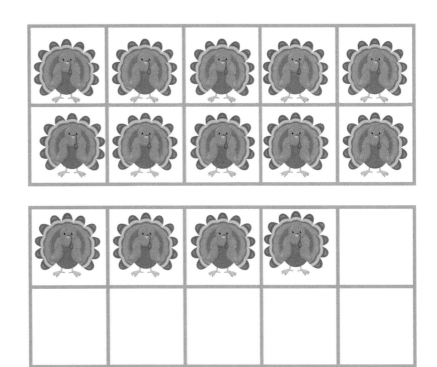

14 14 14

fourteen

HOW MANY RED LEAVES CAN YOU SEE?

15

15 15 15

fifteen

HOW MANY PILGRIMS CAN YOU SEE?

16

16 16 16

sixteen

HOW MANY APPLES CAN YOU SEE?

17

17 17 17

seventeen

HOW MANY FEATHERS CAN YOU SEE?

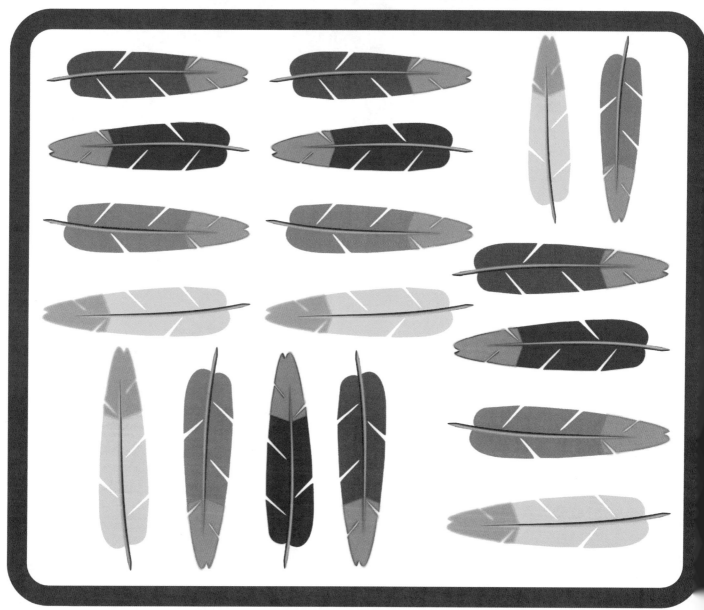

18

18 18 18

eighteen

HOW MANY SUNFLOWERS CAN YOU SEE?

19

19 19 19

nineteen

HOW MANY PUMPKINS CAN YOU SEE?

20

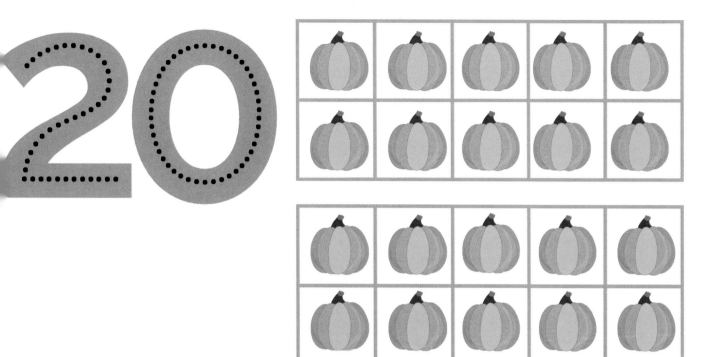

20 20 20
twenty

Happy Thanksgiving!

Made in the USA
Middletown, DE
30 October 2021